At the Farm

Guyla Nelson

and

Saundra Scovell Lamgo

Illustrated by David Grassnick

American Language Series
A Beginning Controlled Vowel Reader

Alpha Omega Publications
Chandler, Arizona

ISBN 0-86717-991-0

For all boys and girls
who wish to
become readers of
good books —
and especially the
Book of Books, the Bible

Stories

The Cat and the Yarn

Mom left a large ball of yarn on the bench.

The cat will knock the yarn off the bench. The yarn will fall on the rug.

As the yarn starts to roll, the cat will grab it. He has a fine time with the soft ball of yarn.

The Month of March

At times the March wind is harsh and cold. At times the March wind is still and calm. The month of March is a fine time to fly a kite.

Frank will fly his kite in the park. He will fly it in the park till dark.

When the stars start to shine, then Frank will pull his kite in from the sky and go home.

2

A Trip on the Barge

The lad made a long trip on a barge. It was a hard trip. Some things on the trip made him sad. He did not want the slaves to have such hard jobs to do. This is why he felt sad.

When this lad got to be a man, much of

his time was spent to help the slaves.

Can we tell the man's name?

A Pet Carp

Carl likes to fish. He has fun when he snags a fat fish. Last month Carl got a big fat carp.

Did Carl take the carp home? Yes, he did, but he did not harm the fish. He did not munch on it when he had lunch. He put the carp in the pond in his back yard.

Carl fed the carp at night. The carp did not starve. The fish ate and ate in the pond. The carp was Carl's fine pet.

6

A Red Scarf

Barb will knit a large red scarf from yarn. She will knit and knit. Barb will use a chart to tell when to start and when to stop.

Part of the scarf will be dark red. Part of the scarf will be light red. It will take a long time to knit the large scarf. It will be a hard job, but Barb will not quit till the scarf is done.

Hit the Mark

We have a fun game. We must hit the mark with a dart. The mark is not large.

Art will start the game. He will toss the dart at the mark. Will he hit it? No, no. He will not hit the mark.

Clark will try next. He will stand quite still. He will think hard. Then he will toss the dart.

Will Clark hit the mark?

Yes, yes! Clark wins the game!

The Swiss Chard

The old man gives Mom a large box of Swiss chard from his farm.

Mom will wash the chard. Then she will use a sharp knife to cut off the bad spots on the chard.

Mom will put part of the chard in a large pan. She will set the pan on the stove.

The rest of the chard Mom will pack in a large jar and mark on the lid—**Swiss Chard**. Then she will give the jar of chard to Miss Marsh.

An Ark in the Nile

This mom has a smart plan. She must hide the babe from the king. She will use large grass stems to make an ark. Then she will pitch the ark with dark, thick tar.

When the ark is dry, this mom will place the babe in the ark. She will set the ark in the marsh so that the tall grass will hide the babe.

She will ask God to let no harm come to the babe. His big sis will stand close by the marsh. She will watch the babe so that no harm comes to him.

When Dogs Bark

Spot and Star are my dogs. The dogs like to run and romp in my back yard. Star thinks it is fun to chase my white cat.

When the dogs bark and bark, I will run to the back yard to check on them.

Why will Spot bark? Spot will bark at the lark.

Why will Star bark? Star will bark at my white cat on the fence.

My dogs will not harm the lark and the cat but will just bark and bark.

My Smart Dad

My dad is smart. God made him smart. My dad can help me do lots of things that are fun.

I love my dad. I will do what my dad tells me to do.

I thank God that He gave me my smart dad.

Stars

God made all the stars and put them in the sky. He gave all the stars a name.

The stars are far from my home. The stars shine and give off light at night. I am glad that the stars make the dark sky bright.

God is smart and wise. God can do big things. I am glad that God made all the stars and put them in the sky.

Gert's Fern

Gert will plant her small fern in a pot. Then she will put the fern in the sun.

God will use the sun to help Gert's fern get big. It will not take a long time.

When her fern gets big, Gert must plant it in a big pot.

God makes her fern get big.

What Nerve!

What nerve Bert has! He went up to the stern clerk and told him to smile. What nerve! Bert was quite brave.

Did the stern clerk smile?

Yes, he did. The clerk gave Bert a big, big smile.

A Terse Verse

Fern wrote a terse verse. She did a fine job when she wrote the verse.

Fern will quote the verse to Mom. Then she will quote the terse verse to Dad. Both Mom and Dad like Fern's verse.

A Verb List

Kerr will make a list. It will be a list of verbs. It will not be long.

Kerr must think and think. On his list he will put these verbs:

       merge   jerk   swerve

Kerr will give his list of verbs to Miss Perth when she comes to class.

Fun to Serve

Gert wakes at six. On her face is a big
smile. She and her mom plan to serve
ham, eggs, rolls, and snacks at a brunch
at ten. Gert's mom has made her a
long dress.

Vern will drive Gert and her mom to the
brunch. Gert is glad she can have on a
long dress. She thinks it is fun to serve.
Her mom will tell her just what to do.

Rose Buds and Fern

I spy a nice fern next to the rocks. I will cut the fern. Then I will place the fern in a glass vase with six rose buds.

I will write a verse on a note pad. I will place the vase with the rose buds and fern next to Mom's plate. When she comes in, she will be glad to find the gift.

Merge Left!

Verle will drive his truck to cut logs. He must get the logs from the high hills. It will be a long trip.

As Verle drives his truck, he will merge to the left at a place by the name of Pine. This place is close to the hills and close to the logs.

Verle will have to swerve his truck to miss the stumps in his path. Then he will go on till he finds lots of logs.

Verle will cut the logs and fill his truck. He will bring the logs back home and stack them in a shed. Then he will split the big logs to make a fire when it gets cold.

A Herd of Swine

When Christ and His men came in a
ship to the land, a sick man ran and
met them.

28

The sick man made his home by the graves. He had no help from his kin. He came to get help from Christ.

Christ made this sick man well. Christ then told the sick man to go and tell what He had done to help him.

A herd of swine fed close by them. When Christ spoke, the herd of swine ran into the lake. Can we tell why?

Quote a Verse

My name is Herb. I want to serve God with my life. My verse will help me serve God. Let me quote my verse—
"In God have I put my trust."

Psalm 56:11

Were We Late?

It is time to go. We must not be late.

Mom still has some things to do. I will help her so that we can go. We must not be late.

As I help Merve, I will quote a verse to him. The verse tells us not to waste time.

Barb's Gifts

Barb was six on the sixth of March. Marge and Clark and Carl came to her back yard.

Marge gave Barb a scarf. Clark gave Barb a red glass jar. The jar was a bank. Carl gave Barb a star charm.

Then Barb and her pals went to ride and swing and slide at the park. What fun on the sixth of March!

33

The Perch

The fish will jerk on the line. Art thinks he will catch a fat perch. The perch is smart.

Art jerks and jerks. At last the perch gets off the line. Art is sad. He did not catch a perch.

But what is this? Is this a prize on his line?

No!
an old,
fern!

Who Made the Kerf?

Who made the kerf on the log?

Was it Charles?

Did he use a sharp ax? Was it a sharp knife that cut the kerf?

I cannot tell who made the kerf, but I think it was made with a sharp knife.

Dad's Old Car

Bert, Herb, and Dad went for a ride in Dad's old car.

"This path has lots of bumps," Bert told Dad.

"Hit the bumps!" spoke Herb.

Did Dad try to hit the bumps?

No! The bumps might harm the tires on his car.

Just then Dad got a glimpse of a large bump in time to swerve the car and miss it.

With a quick jerk, the car went to the
side of the path.

Dad did not hit the bump.

He was glad.

Bert and Herb were sad!

A Stern Kern

Pete likes to have fun. He will go to the park. He will act as if he is a kern. He will march and march. He will be a stern kern.

Pete will make a kerf in the spruce. This kerf is a notch to mark the place of Pete's march.

At last it will be time to go home. Pete must not be a kern at home. He must be a nice lad and not be stern.

Do Not Squirm!

Luke is just a small lad. At times he squirms. He likes to twirl Dad's pen. He likes to whirl first to the left and then to the right.

Mom and Dad want Luke to sit still. Dad wants Luke to face the folks in front of him. He tells Luke to be still and put his hands in his lap.

Mom and Dad must be firm with Luke. Then he will sit still and not squirm. When Luke gets big, he will be glad that Mom and Dad did not shirk the job God gave them.

Thirst

Thirst is a gift from God.

Thirst makes me want to drink. When I get hot, a cold drink will quench my thirst. When I am cold, I like a hot drink. I am glad when God tells me that it is time to get a drink.

I am glad that God tells my pets to get a drink. It is fun to watch them drink.

Thirst is one of God's gifts to me and my pets.

Crumbs on the Ledge

Fred will drop lots of crumbs on the ledge. Then he will watch the birds.

The birds will fly to the ledge. The birds will peck at the crumbs.

When a bird gets full, he will fly to a branch of the fir. He will quench his thirst at the pond.

Then he will fly back to his nest.

Whirl and Swirl

The wind will whirl and swirl the dirt. It will stir up lots and lots of dust. Dirt will get on my face. Dust will get in my nose.

I will run and stand in the shed. When the wind stops, the dirt will not whirl and swirl in my face. Then I can go back to my job.

A Dirge or a Hymn?

A dirge is a sad song. If we sing a dirge, we must not sing it fast. We do not like to sing a dirge, but we do love to sing.

We love to sing old, old hymns. A hymn is a glad song. It tells of God's love and care. A hymn makes us glad.

The Old Kirk

The old kirk is on a high hill. It is a small kirk but is quite nice. A huge birch stands next to the steps of the kirk.

A Scot will come to the kirk. He will take off his hat as he walks up the steps. He will go in the kirk.

Can we tell what a kirk is? A Scot can tell us.

A Bird in the Birch

I spy a small bird. She sits on a high branch of a tall, white birch. Then she hops on the edge of the nest.

The bird sits quite still. She sits on the nest. Eggs are in the nest. The bird will not squirm in the nest. I like to watch the small bird.

The Cart

Clark is a smart lad of ten. He likes to make things. He wants to make a cart for his big dog to pull. Clark wants his cart to be bright red.

Clark must start with pine planks from
the mill. The planks must be the right
length. Dad will use a sharp blade to help
Clark cut them.

Clark will drill holes in the planks. He
will put the pegs in the holes. Then the
planks will be kept in place.

His sharp knife will be a big help.
Clark will carve a star on the side of the
cart. He wants to make the star gold.

At last Barb and Marge will come by.
Will the girls want to have the first ride in
the cart? Yes, and Clark will be glad to
let them be first.

Barb and Marge sit in the cart. It is
fun to have Clark's dog pull the girls in
the cart.

Clark must march in front of the cart.
The girls will have a grand time in the red
and gold cart.

A Bug in a Jar

Dirk went to the park with a jar. He had bits of grass and some sticks and dirt in the jar. The lid of the jar had holes in it. At first Dirk just sat in the thick grass and sang a soft tune.

All at once a black bug lit on a blade of grass in front of him. Dirk was quick to put the jar on top of the bug. He slid the lid on the jar. What a grand catch!

It was not quite dark, and Dirk had to start home. He held the jar in one hand. He did not have a firm grip on the jar. The jar fell. Smash!

The jar broke, but no harm came to the bug. The bug fled into the thick grass as quick as a wink. Dirk put the glass and dirt and sticks in a trash can. He went home fast—with no bug and no jar!

The Smart Dog

Mike has a smart dog. His dog can do lots of tricks.

Mike tells his dog to sit up. He tells his dog to run and fetch the stick. Mike tells his dog to run and catch the stick as it hits the dirt.

Mike's dog is smart. Mike likes his dog. He likes to let his pals watch the tricks that his dog can do.

57

First Grade

This girl is in the first grade. Her name is Ruth. She likes her class. She likes Miss Birch.

Ruth sits still in class. She will not stir. She will not smirk.

Ruth will do what Miss Birch tells her to do. She will do her best.

Chirp! Chirp!

Why will this bird chirp?

He wants to tell us that spring has come.

He will not stir from his perch till he chirps and chirps.

What is the name of this bird with the red chest?

No Dirt on the Shirt

The girl gave the clerk cash. Then the clerk gave the girl a sack. In the sack was a white shirt.

The girl did not have a firm grip on the sack. It fell from her hands, but the shirt did not get dirt on it.

She put the shirt back in the sack and went home with it. Dad was glad that she gave him a white shirt.

The Girl in a White Skirt

These girls first met by the white fence next to the big elm. The girl in the white skirt is Beth. Jane is her pal. Mom just made Beth's skirt. Beth hopes that she will not get dirt on her skirt.

Beth and Jane will walk to the store. Beth wants to find a scarf to match her skirt. Jane will be a big help to Beth.

Beth will give cash to the clerk when she finds the scarf that she likes. Then she and Jane will go home.

63

A Short Form

The man hands Mom a form. Mom must write on the form. It is a form for the bake shop.

Mom must write on the form and tell what kind of tortes she wants. Then she must tell what kind of jam to use in the tortes.

She must tell what time she will come back in the morn to pick up the box of tortes.

Since the form is short, it will not take Mom long to fill it in.

Life in the Dorm

My big sis lives in a dorm. She thinks it is fun to live in a dorm. She is quite at home in the dorm.

In the morn my sis will make up the bunk bed. Then she will sort the notes for a theme that she will write.

The theme Sis will write is of a child who was born in the North. Since the theme will be just a short one, it will not take Sis long to sort the notes.

The Short Man

The short man will climb up on a high branch. He will sit quite still on the branch. He will watch the throng. He will watch for a fine Man to come past. He hopes the Man will not glance at his short form on the high branch.

Who is the fine Man?

He is the Lord. And He spots the short man! The Lord asks the short man to come from the branch. He wants to go home with the short man.

Tell the name of the short man.

A Knife and a Fork

I will place a knife and a fork next to my plate. Then I will place a torte on my plate.

Shall I use my knife or my fork when I cut my torte?

The torte is made from thick, white cake. The torte tastes swell!

York's Horse

York has a horse. York's horse was born last spring. He is still just a colt.

York must not ride his colt yet. He likes to take his horse for a walk on a cold morn.

The colt likes corn mush. York is kind to his horse.

The Bright Torch

This man has a torch. He will light the torch. The flame on the torch is quite bright.

The torch is a fine light for this man. He will use his torch to light his path as he walks or runs.

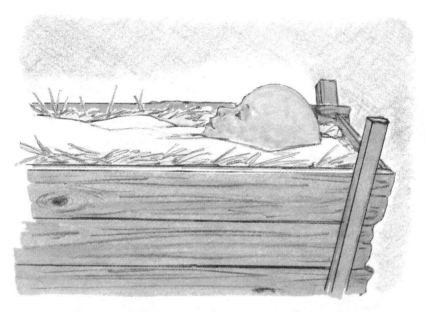

Why Was Christ Born?

A lot of time has gone by since Christ was born. As a Babe, Christ was God's Son. As a Man, He was still God's Son.

As God's Son, Christ hung on the cross for my sin. I love the Lord, God's Son, who was born and then gave His life for me.

A Walk to the Gorge

Stan and I will go for a short walk. We
will take the north path. That path is close
to the gorge.

The gorge is a fine sight. It will be a
nice walk on the north path.

Norm's Corn Patch

Norm will get on his horse. He will go for a ride. The horse will snort as he trots past the chicks and the pigs. Norm will wave to his sis on the back porch.

While Norm rides, he will check his corn patch.

The corn is not short. God sent the hot sun to make the corn get tall.

Norm likes to watch the corn go up, up, up. He is glad that he can ride his horse to check his corn patch.

The Red Car

Dad gave me a small red car. It can go far when I push it or pull it.

Last night I left my car in the front yard. Carl got it for me. He put my car on the front porch.

I am glad that no one stole my car. When I go in my home, I must take my small car with me. Then it will be safe!

The Gold Harp

Lots of strings stretch on the large frame of this gold harp. Since its tones are not sharp or harsh, this girl likes the tones.

The strings of her harp are strong. She must work hard to pluck the right strings with her hands to get the tones she wants. Skill on the harp comes with time and hard work.

This smart girl charms us as she plucks a soft tune. We like her harp, and we like her songs.

Zeb

Zeb was born in the North. He still lives there. It is quite cold where Zeb lives. The wind is strong and cold. Lots of ice and soft white flakes are on the land.

Zeb lives in an ice home. He must have thick, warm clothes. He must have these on all the time since his home is quite cold.

Zeb likes the cold and ice. He likes to fish. He likes to watch the white flakes drop from the sky. Can we tell what these flakes are? Zeb is glad that he lives in the North.

The Stork

The stork is big. She has long, long legs. She has a long neck. The stork can twist her long neck, or she can hold her neck quite still.

The big stork makes a fine nest. She sits on the nest a long time. She sits on the nest from morn till night.

At last a small babe is born. The stork is small and thin. The small stork has a long, thin neck and long, long legs. God made both storks.

Merle and Verle

The twins were sick and had to rest in bed. Both Merle and Verle had colds. Mom came in to serve them a snack.

Merle and Verle were glad for the snack and told Mom, "Thanks!" The twins gave thanks to God for the snack.

Next Mom will talk to God and ask Him to make Merle and Verle well. God is a kind God. God can make the twins well. He is glad when we talk to Him. When we are sick, God can make us well.

A Quick Storm

Mom sent me to the store for her. I was to ask the clerk for a cork, some forks, and some corn.

While I was in the store, a storm came up. I had to run fast to my home. I did not stop, but I got a bit wet. My short, tan sack got quite wet. I was glad the store was not far from my home.

A Game with the Wind

It was morn when the lad sat on the porch. He sat on a bench with his horn. His mind was on his songs. He sat and made soft tones with his horn.

A storm was close. The north wind came in huge gusts. All at once the lad felt the wind go past. With the wind went his songs! He ran to try to catch them.

Just as the lad bent to pick up a song, the wind made it jerk from his hands. One song fell in a fern close by the porch. He got that song!

The wind made one song swerve from the lad and land by the herd of swine. It went far, and the lad did not find it.

The wind had lots of fun in this game with the lad.

A Gift for Sis

Charles is a clerk in the gift store. He is nice and kind. He is not stern. He sells gifts.

Marge stops in the store to get a gift for her sis. Charles will help Marge pick a nice fern.

Then he will help Marge find a red pot just the right size to hold the fern.

The pot that Marge likes has a star on the side.

Charles will help Marge plant the fern in the red pot. Marge thanks Charles for his help.

She thinks her sis will like this nice gift.

Pals

Bert and Jim are pals. These pals will go for a ride on the bikes.

Lambs stand or sit in the path of the bikes. The lads will have to swerve to miss the flock of lambs.

Bert and Jim are glad that the bikes did not hit the lambs.

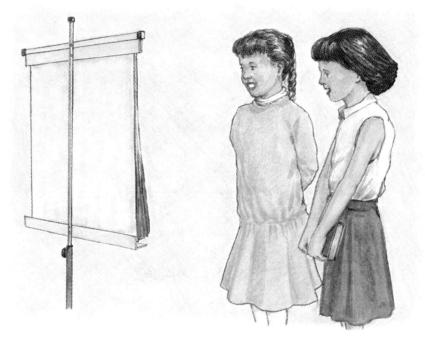

What Not to Do!

Jill and Grace came to class. These words were on the chart by Miss Horn's desk:

I will not mar my desk.

Grace made a quick glance at Jill. Jill had a squint on her face.

"I will not mar my desk?" Jill spoke in a soft tone. "I hope Miss Horn tells us what we are not to do!"

"We must not write on the desk tops. We must not scratch the desks. We must not carve names on the desks," spoke Miss Horn at last.

Then Grace told Jill and the class, "This desk is not mine. The desk is for me to use. I must take care of it. I think I can tell what it is to mar a desk."

All of the class then wrote these words on note pads—

I will not mar my desk.

Will the Ship Sink?

The men got in a ship to fish on the lake. When the nets were cast, a bad storm came up. Strong wind made the ship whirl and twirl and toss in the high waves.

Will the ship sink? The ship might sink! The men are sad and cry for help. Watch!

A Man comes to them. He stands on the waves. It is the Lord! The Lord is God.

The Lord will help them. He will save them. He is kind.

The Lord will help us. We must ask Him for help.

Hark! Hark! A Lark!

Art and Marge sat in the front yard close to a tall spruce. Marge sat quite still. Art was first to note the lark. Her perch was on a limb of the spruce.

"I spy a lark," Art spoke in a soft tone.

"Hark! Hark! I think that lark will make a nest!" Art told Marge.

"I hope she will make a nice nest," spoke Marge. "That will be fun to watch. Will it take a long time?"

"I think it will," Art spoke a third time. "She has to go far to get twigs and grass and bits of yarn. Some of these she will find at the barn. Some she will find by the marsh."

"I hope her mate will help her," Marge told Art with a sigh. "That must be a hard job!"

"I am sure he will. God made birds to do just the right things to help," Art told Marge.

"Here he comes!" Marge spoke. "We will watch them work as long as we can till it gets dark."

Left on Third Base!

"It is fun to hit the ball," spoke Jake to his pal, Ward Knox. "I must try hard to hit the ball far from home plate. It will take lots of hard work."

"I like to get past first base when I hit the ball," spoke Ward.

Then Jake told Ward, "It is fun to make it to third base, but it is no fun to be left on third! When I get big, I will hit the ball far and make a home run!"

Yarn for Sale

Mom sent Gert to the knit shop last month. It was not far, but Gert drove Dad's black car. The knit shop had a huge sale of yarn. The price was not large since all yarn was on sale.

Gert chose red and black and white yarn. She got nine balls of red yarn, five balls of black yarn, and six balls of white yarn. Gert gave cash to the clerk. The clerk put the yarn in a large bag. Gert drove home with the yarn and gave it to her mom.

Gert wants her mom to knit a red vest with a scarf, a hat, and gloves to match. Mom will knit some black stripes and some white stripes on the hat. The vest will have stripes at the neck and at the arms. She will knit stripes on the gloves and on the scarf.

It will not be hard work for Gert's mom. She likes to knit. She will wind the yarn with care so that it will not snarl.

Gert will be warm in her hat, vest, scarf, and gloves. She will thank her mom. Gert plans to make a warm red skirt to match.

Fun to Ride

Art and Bert think it is fun to ride the horse. The lads will go on the horse to a farm that is far from home.

The horse will run part of the time and walk part of the time. It will be dark when Art and Bert start for home, but the sky will be bright with stars. Dogs will bark at them, but the horse will trot fast.

106

Bert will bring home a bag full of nuts. He plans to parch them by the fire on cold nights. Art will have a sack of chard, a box of squash, and a jar of plum jam.

It will not take long to wash the chard and fix it in a pan. Mom and Sis will bake the squash to serve with the hot rolls and jam. Art and Bert will not starve!

Snack by the Shore

Arch and Mort ate a snack by the shore. The bench on which Arch sat was white with red stripes. Mort's bench was tan with black stripes. It was fun to sit and watch the waves while the lads ate.

A kind old man came to serve them. Arch had perch on a bun. Mort had a hot dog and a cold drink. Arch spoke first, "Let us thank the Lord."

The lads ate for just a short time. It was fun to watch the small fish jump. No shark or whale came close to the shore!

God Made the Wind!

The limbs of the birch dip and rise. The strong wind shakes the birch. The tall grass bends as a strong gust of wind comes up. Bits of trash fall here and there.

George and Carl like the wind. These lads think it is fun to run in the wind.

Birds like the wind. Some birds sit on a high perch. Some birds chirp and chirp in the brisk wind.

We cannot tell where the wind comes from. We cannot tell where the wind will go. But this we can tell—God made the wind!

Curt and His Bike

Curt likes to ride his bike. He likes to ride his bike to church. He rides next to the curb. He thinks it is safe next to the curb.

Curt will watch to the right and to the left when he makes a turn. Curt takes the curve quite fast. He falls from his bike! Curt is not hurt, but he will be late to church!

Do Right

I will do right. I will not curse. It is a sin to curse. It hurts God. It hurts me. It hurts my mom and dad.

Since I love God, I will be sure that I do not blurt things which make Him sad. I will urge my chums not to curse. When we talk, we will make sure that we do right.

The Kind Man

A man came to the small burg. He was kind. He was not curt. He went from home to home in the small burg. His plan was to urge those with whom he spoke to come to church with him. He told them of God's love.

This kind man had a task to do. He did not stop till he had gone to all the homes in the burg.

The Can of Pop

Tim has a can of pop. The can is hot. Dad will urge Tim not to shake the can. If the can bursts, then pop will spurt from the can. Tim will get wet, and he might get hurt.

Tim must not let the can burst. When the pop is cold, Tim will lift the lid and drink the pop.

Who is He?

He has soft fur. His fur is white. His home is on the farm. At times he hops to the church yard to munch on grass. He is shy. He runs and hides when we come to church.

I like to watch him turn and run from us. Can we tell who he is?

Walk in his tracks to find him!

Here he is on the farm
by the fence.

A Fine Lunch

Watch the cat lurk by the urn. He will be quite still as he hides there. Why must the cat lurk?

The cat must watch since the mice might come past the urn. Then the cat will burst from the side of the urn. He will catch the mice. Then he will have a fine lunch.

The Turf Farm

Curt and Bart will go with Dad to the turf farm. Dad must have turf to sod the back yard. The lads are not sure what a turf farm is!

The farm is not far from home. Dad will turn at the curve just past the old church. Then he will drive five miles to the farm.

The man who runs the turf farm will let the lads go with him to get the turf. The lads find rolls and rolls of turf. Curt stands next to a large stack of turf by the fence. Some rolls of turf are in the barn.

Curt and Bart will help take the rolls of turf to Dad's truck. Since the rolls are not light, the lads take just one roll at a time. Dad and the man are strong and can lift more than one roll at a time. The men and the lads work hard. It takes a long time to fill the truck with turf.

It was fun to go to the turf farm. The turf
will make a nice sod for the back yard. It
will be hard work to put the turf there.

Purr! Purr!

My cat has soft, tan fur. I like to stroke her fur. Her fur is nice and soft.

My cat gets close to my legs. She likes to purr.

I will not hurt my cat. She is my pet.

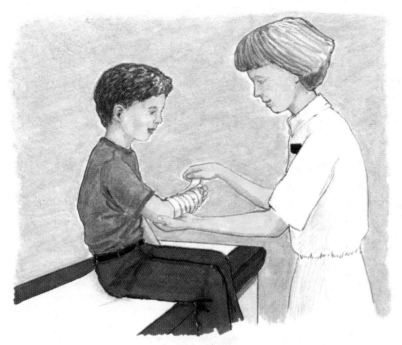

Bert

Bert fell on his arm. His arm is hurt. He cannot turn it.

Bert will go to the nurse. She will check his arm. Then she will wrap his arm.

The nurse will not hurt Bert. She will be kind to Bert. Bert thinks the nurse is nice.

124

The Black Serge

The clerk takes a bolt of black serge from the high shelf. "Is this the kind of cloth, Miss Murch?"

"Yes, I think that cloth will be fine. It is thick and will be warm. It will last a long time."

Miss Murch gets some cash from her purse and hands it to the clerk. He puts five yards of the serge in a bag, and she takes the cloth home.

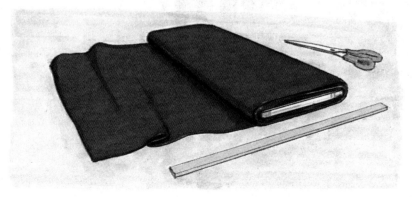

Will the Car Start?

Sam likes Dad's red car. Dad got it last
March at a shop not far from home.

When the wind is cold at night, the car is hard to start the next morn. Dad parks his red car in a shed close to the barn on cold nights. Then it will start the next morn, and he will not have to scrape off the ice!

Mom likes to drive Dad's red car. Sam likes to ride with Mom. She will start the car and drive it to a store. She wants starch, lard, jars, and a sharp knife. Sam will help Mom get these things.

Fun with Dad

It is hot. Jeff and Rob are in the back yard. The lads watch as Dad turns on the hose by the front gate.

Dad will watch as Jeff and Rob come to the gate. Dad whirls and twirls the hose. It squirts on Jeff and Rob.

Jeff and Rob squirm as the hose gets them in the face and arms.

Jeff runs to the birch to hide. Rob runs and jumps up on the fence. Dad likes to squirt his sons. Jeff and Rob have fun!

Just a Small Spark

A big fire in the park! The birch and the fir are in the path of the fire. These will be quick to burn. Smoke and flames are in this huge park.

The smoke churns and churns in the sky. Men work hard to try to stop the fire, but it still burns. Most of the land will be black. The fox must find a home. The birds must find homes.

We must use care when we camp in the park. Just a small spark from a fire at my camp can start a big fire.

He Kept the Purse

The man has a task. It is his job to take care of the purse. All the men trust this man with the change in the purse. The men think this man is kind and loves God.

But this man who takes care of the purse will hurt the Lord. He will spurn this Man. He will help bad men get this Man hung on a cross. He will turn from those that love him. He will do wrong.

Can we name the man who kept the purse?

Corn for the Pigs

Mort has lots of pigs. The pigs are in a pen at the north end of his land. He must make sure that he will not run short of corn for his pigs.

Mort will fill the back of his truck with corn. When his truck is full, Mort will drive to the pen.

One pig was born just this morn. That pig will not get corn. He will get his milk from his mom.

135

We Go to Church

I like to go to church. Mom curls my long locks. I put on my best dress. I take God's Word with me.

Herb likes to go to church. He will sit next to me. I will let him share God's Word.

We both like church.

What Is a Tarn?

Brad spoke to Vern and me one morn with a big smile. "I think that lads who are nine might like to fish at the tarn by North Park and pull in some big fish."

"Right, Brad, but what is a tarn?"

"A tarn is a lake in the high hills. It is the best place to fish," Brad told us. "Most of the time the tarn has ice on it. When the ice melts, we can hike to the tarn. We can climb the high bank of this lake and catch lots of big fish. Want to go with me?"

"Must he urge us?" I spoke to Vern. "I will pack my bags at once."

Lots of Thorns

The rose bush is close to the porch. Deb wants to cut a rose bud from the bush. The bush has lots of thorns on it. What will Deb do?

She will try not to prick her thumb. She will use a sharp knife. Then she will put the rose bud in a vase. The bud will look nice in the vase.

The Torn Shirt

Merle fell off the porch. He hit his arm on a large rock. The rock tore his shirt and made a gash in his arm. Merle was sad. He was hurt. He had worn his nice shirt just for a short time.

Mom will be stern! She will scold Merle for his torn shirt. She had told him to put on an old shirt. Merle felt bad. He had not done what Mom had told him.

Can Mom mend the shirt? We hope she can. Can God mend the arm? Yes, He can, and He will.

Nine Rules to Live By

1. I will not shirk my job.
2. I will not jerk things from my pals.
3. I will not slurp my broth from the cup.
4. I will not burp.
5. I will not gorge my lunch.
6. I will not let sin scar my life.
7. I will not spurn God's love.
8. I will let God be my Lord.
9. I will serve God all of my life.

143

Did It Scorch?

Marsh wants to help Fran make fudge. He thinks she will let him taste it.

First, Marsh and Fran crack the nuts and chop them. Marsh gets a pan for Fran.

She adds milk to the things in the pan and puts the pan on the stove. Marsh will stir and stir while the pan of fudge gets hot. He will not let it scorch if he stirs it. Fran will not want the fudge to burn.

The fudge must be just right. Fran will test it in a cup to be sure it is done. Then she will stir it hard and fast till it gets a bit thick. At just the right time, Fran will add the nuts and turn the fudge onto a plate.

When the fudge gets cold, Fran will cut it into squares. She will serve Marsh the first bite!

Yum, yum! Marsh likes the fudge. It did not scorch!

What Is a Verb?

A verb is to be or to do.

Here are some verbs to write on the note pads:

carve

serve

squirt

scorch

hurt

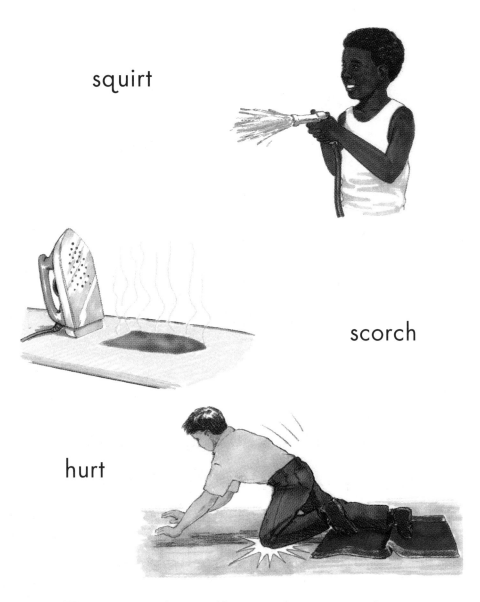

These verbs tell us what we do.

147

Dare to Be Brave

The brave man was far from home in a strange land. It was not the land of his birth, yet the man was brave. He spoke, "I will serve God in this strange land. He is still my God!"

As the sun came up in the morn, the man knelt and spoke with his God. When it was time for lunch, he knelt and spoke with God. As the sun set, he spoke with God for the third time.

Men who were not kind told the king
that the man knelt and spoke to his God.
The king told the men to warn the brave
man that he must stop, but the brave man
still knelt and spoke to God. He did not
try to hide.

The king was sad, but he had the brave man cast into a huge, dark den. The den was full of wild cats.

Did God spare the brave man? Yes, God made the wild cats to be like pets. The big cats did not harm him as he slept right next to them. God kept the man safe.

March in the Square

It is a bright, warm morn. Men march in the square of the small burg. The men stand tall and hold the guns high.

Watch these men march to the tune of the fife and drum.

These brave men fight for what is right for this land. The men will not quit but will fight hard. The men hope that no harm will come to this land.

God's World

God made the world. Right from the start He had a plan. At first all was dark and black. Then God spoke just the word and there was light. He spoke and there was the large, bright sun in the sky to light the morn. Then He spoke the word and there were stars to light the dark night sky.

It was not hard for God to make the
world. He had a plan for all that He made.
And all was put in just the right place.

The frogs, the worms, the bugs, and the
snakes were all made by God.

The larks and the wrens were made
by God.

God made the horse, the dog, the cat, the hare, and all pets to share with us.

Fish, clams, crabs, and sharks were part of all that God made for the world.

Then God made the first man from dust.
From the man's rib He made a wife. She
was to be a help to him.

God loves and cares for all that He made
in the world. He loves and cares for us.

A Brave Man

He sat tall on his white horse as he led his men in war. He was brave and strong. He had led his men well in the long war.

His plans were for the birth of a fine, strong land when the war was done. It was his wish for men to do right and to stand strong for God.

Tell the man's name.

The Worn Page

She is old, yet she shares God's Word with me. She loves the Lord so much that she spends much of her time in His Word.

One page is quite worn. On that page is the psalm which she likes best. It tells that her help comes from God. I am glad that she shares this psalm with me.

I hope that I will love God's Word just as much when I am old.

159

Sis Helps Mom

Sis will help Mom with the work at home. First, Mom wants Sis to help her make tart plum jam. It is fun to watch the jam swirl in the pan. Sis must stir the jam fast. It must not stick to the big pan. She must not let it scorch or burn. When the jam is done, Sis will store it in glass jars.

Next Sis must help Mom press the clothes. Mom tells Sis to use care. She must not scorch Dad's shirts and pants. She must not shirk her work.

A Rare Pin

"I like the pin on that dress," Miss Jones told Barb.

"Thanks," spoke Barb. "Dad got this rare pin for me at a small shop on the north side of Rome. It is a nice gift and just fits my taste. I think it makes my black dress quite sharp."

"What makes this a rare pin?" Miss Jones spoke once more.

"The old man at the shop told Dad that this pin is one of a kind. When a man carves by hand from this white rock, no pin is just like the next pin that he carves. Dad tells me that things made by hand will

not be just the same. This makes them rare
and might make them worth more cash.

When this old man can carve no more
pins, the work of his hands will be scarce.
I will then be quite glad that Dad got this
rare pin for me."

Bare Limbs

So tall the elm stands! What a sight as its bare limbs stretch high into the sky!

Dad hung a thick rope from one of the huge bare limbs. Then he put a big knot in the rope to hold the tire in place. What a fine swing it made!

Last spring the elm made a fine home for the lark. The lark was smart to make her nest on a high branch. But when it got cold and the limbs were bare, the bird did not care to make her home there. She and her babes left. The bare limb was not safe for them.

The Man Who Hid from God

The man had a plan. His plan was to hide from God.

But the man did not hide from God. The man got on a large ship. He went on a trip. Did God watch what the man did on the ship? Yes, God did watch him.

The sky got dark. God sent huge waves and strong, harsh winds. The men on the ship felt that the ship might sink. The ship was far, far from land. The men went to the man and woke him from his nap.

The man spoke, "I cannot hide from God. God has sent the strong winds. God is sad with me. I must not try to hide

from God. Just push me from the ship,
and the harsh winds will stop."

   The men were sad. It was a hard thing
that the man told them to do. But the men
did not want the ship to sink. The men did
as the man had told them.

But God was with the man. God sent a
huge fish in the dark night. The fish made
a big gulp, and the man was safe in the
fish. The men on the ship were safe, and
God made the harsh winds stop.

At last God told the large fish to spit up the man. Then the man was on the land. He did not want to hide. He was quick to do what God had told him to do. Who was this man? God's Word tells us.

The Mare and Her Colt

Late last night Dad went to the barn to check on Star, his black mare. He ran back home fast. "Where is my torch?" he spoke with a short gasp.

Dan ran to the back porch to get the torch. "What is it for?" Dan spoke and gave the torch to his dad at the same time.

"Want to come with me? Come and we will take a squint at Star's black colt," Dad told Dan and Dave with a huge smile. "The torch will light the barn and help us check on Star's colt. We must be sure the colt is fine."

"There he is next to the mare!" spoke Dave. "He is not big. He is short, and his legs are not strong yet."

Dad told the lads, "We must not move fast and scare him or the mare. Just stand back here and get a nice glimpse of them."

Star made a short snort, but Dad was
kind to her. He let Dan and Dave watch
while he fed her some nice corn. Dad
gave her a warm drink from a big tub. It
was time for the colt to get his milk and a
nap. Then Dad and the lads went back
home for the night.